Lee Abbey. Lynton.

Tea Cottage Cookery Book

Oh, taste and see that the LORD is good.

PSALM 34:8

Dedication

This book is dedicated to all the people who have ever
served on the Community at Lee Abbey.

Lee Abbey
Christian Community

Lynton North Devon EX35 6JJ

Lee Abbey Fellowship Registered Charity No. 1094097

Tel: 01598 752621 Web: www.leeabbey.org.uk/devon

Email: relax@leeabbey.org.uk

Compiled by Pixie Paris Rowe © 2013
Published by Lee Abbey 2013

ISBN 978-0-9926201-0-3

The mark of responsible forestry www.fsc.org

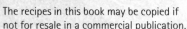

The recipes in this book may be copied if
not for resale in a commercial publication.

Illustration:
Sarah Prentice

Photography:
Designpics.com, Melissa Baker, Andrew Mann, Sarah Prentice,
Jamie Robinson, Pixie Rowe, Sally Scyner.

Art editor:
Sarah Prentice www.sarahprenticedesign.co.uk

All profits from the sale of this book go to the Lee Abbey Bursary Fund

Lee Abbey Devon offers a unique setting
for time out to relax, be refreshed
and renewed. This is served by our
International Christian Community who
live, pray, eat and work alongside each
other, welcoming everyone who God
sends to us as guests. The Lee Abbey
Bursary Fund makes it possible for many
folk to come and enjoy the hospitality
of Lee Abbey Devon who could not
otherwise afford it and provides a
vital support particularly for those in
extra need of a break. Thank you for
contributing to this important work by
purchasing this Cookery Book.

All enquiries about the Bursary Fund
can be made to the Warden of Lee Abbey
Devon. Email: warden@leeabbey.org.uk

Contents

Introduction

SINCE IT WAS FOUNDED IN 1946, the Lee Abbey Devon Christian Community and their guests have gathered for food and fellowship and probably drunk over ten million cups of tea! Being God's welcome includes sustenance, both physical and spiritual. This could be a cup of tea in the gallery overlooking the astonishingly beautiful Lee Bay, a meal in the dining room served by the International Community members, or just an open gate and well tended path of flowers at the Tea Cottage on an early summer's day.

A taste of heaven in Devon

It is not surprising that other Lee Abbey cookery books have been produced before this one. People like to know what goes on behind the scenes, both at the Tea Cottage and in the main Conference, Retreat and Holiday Centre. This little book looks at some of the actual Tea Cottage recipes and some of the stories that make up the life and times of Lee Abbey Devon. Thousands of visitors, Community members, summer campers, walkers and local folk who come along each have their own memories of this incredible patch of God's earth. For many, the photos, the history, or the tastes, might evoke a

'Thousands of visitors ... who come along each have their own memories of this incredible patch of God's earth.'

picture of being in a very special place known as Lee Abbey.

Shopping choices

Food is about the people who grow it, cook it and share it with those around them as well as nutritional balance. If we never had celebration food, life would be the poorer for it. I can bear witness that a cream tea every day makes you fat; however, once in a while on holiday it is a blessing to enjoy! Mostly food is something for which we can be very thankful to God and enjoy to his praise and glory. If we get to know and care more about the lives of those who produce the raw material going into our food, even better. Our choices make a big difference when we shop. That goes for struggling British farmers as well as seriously impoverished agricultural workers in developing countries.

Weights and measures: some practical pointers for using the recipes

Measurements and ingredients, terms and tastes vary everywhere, even within countries. What we call a cooker and table in the UK, is known as a stove and a counter in Washington State, where I grew up. Now that I have lived in England for longer than I did my native USA, I have tried to learn metric weights and measures, but I am still not sure when a pan is a pot or a can is a tin.

Sometimes this all becomes a non-issue when I am cooking with people from Germany, Poland, Czech Republic, Russia or Brazil, because all I need to say is: 'Put this dough on these'. If you are not using this book in the United Kingdom and Elizabeth II is not on your throne, then all the best and send us an email for help!

I have listed (lb) pounds and (oz) ounces as dry weight on the recipes alongside metric and when it is fluid ounces, (fl oz) it states fluid. (The British use weighing scales for baking/cooking.) It is probably easier to just convert and use these rather than try and adapt to US cups for these recipes. Scales are widely available as they are part of many diet

programmes. The British pint and American quarts don't get a look in, I have just listed ounces (oz) as that covers both sides of the Atlantic, or those who may be far from home. It is important to just use one set of measurements, either metric or imperial, not a mixture of both when using any of these recipes.

Tablespoons and teaspoons – if we all use ones specifically for this purpose from a cookery shop and all are level, we should be just fine.

Ingredients

Eggs – none of these recipes will fail if a few larger ones are used. We usually base the recipes on medium size, free range eggs from Cobley Farms, nearby. I know some people weigh the eggs once broken and then, for example, in sponge cakes, weigh the sugar, fat and flour the same as the eggs weigh.

Clotted cream – Europeans and Americans will just have to come over here to enjoy it, until someone outside the UK understands it enough to make it properly! Heavy whipped cream will do, but it is not the same.

Vanilla – is a vital ingredient. It is worth getting the best you can, obviously Fairtrade would be ideal. Someone has to grow those vanilla beans! You could also buy some whole vanilla pods, cut them open and use the gooey seeds from inside, using a sharp small knife just scrape them all out. Then put the remaining pods in with your caster sugar to add a subtle flavour of joy.

Coriander – is known as cilantro in the States.

Sugar – The various sugars listed in recipes are mostly interchangeable except icing sugar, you just get a very different taste and texture. American all-purpose flour is closest to British plain flour. Have fun with these recipes and give it a go.

Preparing tins for baking

We use oil spray on baking trays, cake pans and muffin tins. This is less messy and cuts the overall fat used. Good baking parchment also saves washing up and protects the bases of things somewhat from burning whilst baking.

Oven temperatures

I have listed three types of oven temperatures, but every oven is different and fan ovens are another thing again. Use common sense and pray.

Fairtrade

If an ingredient is available fairly traded, I have listed FT after the item. If a product is in shops everywhere as Fairtrade it is hoped people will choose Fairtrade items, so I have listed them as such.

Hopefully, by the time this goes to print, even more products will be readily available as certified

Judy from Germany and Alex from the UK, former members of the Tea Cottage Team

Fairtrade. For more details, go to **www.fairtrade.org.uk**

Contributors

The contributions to this book are many and due to the constantly renewing nature of the Lee Abbey Community and its international membership, as soon as this goes to print, many of the people involved may have moved on to pastures new. I have chosen to attempt to draw all these threads together, as it is about the middle of our time here in Devon. Cathy Park has taken up the leadership of the Tea Cottage Team now and the fine tradition of a lovely cream tea in the most incredible setting continues here at Lee Abbey. Several of Cathy's own recipes are included here for us all.

David and Pixie Rowe

David leads the Community and is known as the Warden. My role has included helping run the conference centre shop, adding a Fairtrade shop at the Tea Cottage, overseeing the Tea Cottage for four seasons and assisting with the decor of the main house.

Before we joined the Community, David was a Rector, Diocesan Advisor in Evangelism and Chaplain of a Church of England secondary school in Nottingham, England. I was a partner/director of Grace and Flavour (Nottingham) Limited, a catering business, with friends Sue and Roger Periam. My involvement with Fairtrade overlapped with this foodie work and continues now at Lee Abbey. We have four nearly all grown up children and a darling granddaughter. They are often working and sharing alongside us in Devon and love food too! They have taught me a great deal about cooking, having fun and loving God.

Cakes & Cookies

White Chocolate and Raspberry Cookies

Makes 20–30 cookies

Preheat oven to 180°C (350°F) Gas 4

Baking trays sprayed with oil or lined with baking parchment

225g (8oz) unsalted butter, softened

225g (8oz) caster sugar FT

170g tin condensed milk

350g (12oz) self raising flour

150g (5½oz) white chocolate FT, chopped

175g (6oz) fresh raspberries

White Chocolate and Raspberry Cookies

🐝 In a large bowl, cream the butter and sugar until pale and then stir in the condensed milk. Sift in the flour and then work into a soft dough with your hands. Mix in the chocolate.

🐝 Take a small handful of dough and flatten with your fingers. Place 2–3 raspberries into the centre of the cookie and fold over the sides of the dough to encase the raspberries. Repeat with the remaining dough.

🐝 Place onto parchment lined baking trays, spacing well apart and bake for about 15–18 minutes or until golden brown at the edges, but still a little soft.

🐝 Leave to cool slightly and set before transferring to a cooling rack.

🐝 The dough without the raspberries will keep in the fridge for two-three days or for about one month in the freezer. Freeze in small slightly flattened chunks and bake as required.

Scottish Tablet or Lee Abbey Tea Cottage Fudge

Oven tin lined with parchment and buttered/sprayed with oil

Glass of cold water for testing 'soft ball stage'

900g (2lb)
granulated sugar FT

125g (4oz) butter

150ml (5fl oz) water

150ml (5fl oz) milk

large tin of
condensed milk 397g

1 teaspoon of
vanilla essence FT

Scottish Tablet or Lee Abbey Tea Cottage Fudge

🍎 Put the sugar, butter, water and milk into a large, heavy pan over a low heat and stir until the sugar has completely dissolved.

🍎 Bring to the boil and boil for 10 minutes without stirring. Stir in the condensed milk and boil for a further 10 minutes.

🍎 Remove from heat and add the essence. Beat the mixture for about 5 minutes, then pour into a tin and mark into squares. Cut when cold. (Test to see if cooked enough by dropping a small amount into cold water; if it forms a ball, it is ready.)

🍎 Hannah K Rowlinson says: begin to beat on the cooker first; add vanilla after 3 or 4 minutes, don't put on a cold surface too soon when beating, as this seems to reduce white lines appearing in the finished fudge.

🍎 This can be flavoured with ginger, or chopped nuts added. Peppermint works well too – add instead of vanilla essence. We often serve small portions of this on the side of each hot drink at the Tea Cottage.

Although we have many requests to sell it, it doesn't keep very long, so we just keep giving it away with a smile.

Our thanks go to Harriet Rowbotham Byatt, former Tea Cottage Team member, for the introduction to this sugary treat.

Helen's Fair Honey Flapjacks from *Fair's Fair*

Preheat oven to 190°C (375°F) Gas 5

Grease a 25.5cm (10 x 10in) tin

225g (8oz) margarine

4 level dessert spoons of honey FT

225g (8oz) demerara sugar FT

350g (12oz) rolled oats

100g dairy-free chocolate FT (optional)

Helen's Fair Honey Flapjacks

🍎 Melt margarine and honey together gently in a pan.

🍎 Stir in sugar and oats, off the heat.

🍎 Spread evenly in the tin and bake for about 20 minutes until golden brown.

🍎 Allow to cool slightly before cutting into squares and leave in the tin until cold. Store in an airtight tin, or the flapjacks can be frozen. Also nice topped with a drizzle of melted dairy-free Fairtrade chocolate. These are dairy and wheat-free but not gluten-free.

Note: *we also make flapjack with gluten-free oats, available from larger supermarkets and whole food shops. You might want to experiment with this, as some GF oats are very sharp-edged and make a very gritty flapjack. Top with lots of Fairtrade chocolate.*

Thank you to Helen Durant of Fair's Fair in Barnstaple, Devon, for this recipe and support.

Brownies in a Roasting Tin

Preheat oven to 180°C (350°F) Gas 4

In a large roasting tin

28 x 34cm (11 x 13in) or near this size

Spray with oil and double line the tin with baking parchment, preferably with tall sides to prevent overflow and oven cleaning.

200g (8oz)
dark chocolate FT

440g (1lb) butter

900g (2lb) caster sugar

200g (8oz) plain flour

4 teaspoons baking powder

1 teaspoon salt

8 eggs, beaten

2 teaspoons vanilla essence FT

These can be made dairy-free with vegan margarine. Check your chocolate is vegan and dairy-free too.

Brownies in a Roasting Tin

Melt together the chocolate and butter over simmering water but don't let the water boil, as then it **cooks** the chocolate, which is not a good thing ...

Add the remaining ingredients – eggs last.

Spread in the tin that is double lined and up the sides (this helps prevent burning and makes it easy to lift out when cooled). The brownies are done when they have risen and gone back down; about 30-35 minutes. They will be starting to pull away from the sides and will not wobble.

Don't over-cook, they are meant to be softer than chocolate cake, but not too gooey to cut into squares! Shame, if they were undercooked, then you'd have to spoon them out straight into your mouth. Sigh.

Cool before cutting. These are amazing served slightly warm with clotted cream or, as often served in the main house, with vanilla ice cream.

Whole Oat Fair Fruit Slice

Preheat oven 180°C (350°F) Gas 4

Line your largest roasting tin or two small ones with baking parchment

900g (2lb) of dried fruit FT

1 litre (35fl oz) of fruit juice FT

300g (12oz) whole oats (porridge oats will do)

300g (12oz) plain flour

175g (6oz) brown sugar FT

3 teaspoons baking powder

2 teaspoons ground cinnamon FT

300g (12oz) margarine

Vegan, dairy-free, egg-free.

Whole Oat Fair Fruit Slice

- Soak the dried fruit (dates, apricots, raisins, cranberries, blueberries, mango, sultanas, figs, pineapple, pears, apples, etc.) in one litre of fruit juice.

- Stir over a low heat until the juice is absorbed.

- Put all the dry ingredients in a bowl and add the margarine.

- Use a mixer on a low/medium speed until completely blended or by hand as for pastry.

- Press half the mixture over your tin and press hard to cover every bit. Top with plumped-up fruit, then sprinkle the rest of oat mixture over the top of both and **press down**. Try using a piece of baking parchment to press down, to avoid fruity fingers!

- Bake for about 30 minutes. Cool in tins and cut.

- This keeps very well for about a week and can be frozen. High in fibre and yummy. You can feature a single fruit, such as dates or apricots FT, but a mixture is fun, useful for using up bits and adds variety. Also nice with ginger added, such as in syrup – chopped and added to the fruit with a little of the syrup.

Tiffin

(No-bake and very easy with nearly all Fairtrade ingredients)

Large saucepan or stock pan

Line a tray with baking parchment or greaseproof paper, preferably one that fits in your fridge. About 21 x 27cm (8 x 10.5in)

750g (1lb 10oz) crushed digestive biscuits – shop ones or try Fairtrade whole wheat digestives (from Traidcraft)

200g (8oz) dark chocolate FT

2 handfuls in total of cranberries/sultanas, cherries, raisins, etc. FT

250g (9oz) butter/margarine

2 tablespoons golden syrup FT

1 teaspoon vanilla essence FT

Plus more chocolate FT for topping

Tiffin

🍒 Melt the chocolate, butter and golden syrup, add the fruit and when melted, add the digestives.

🍒 Press very firmly into a lined tray, try using a piece of parchment to avoid chocolate hands (unless of course you **want** that) and chill for several hours.

🍒 To finish add chocolate drops on top (50g) or drizzle with white Fairtrade chocolate and sprinkle with crumbled bits of fudge. You could easily make this dairy-free with vegan margarine, dark dairy-free chocolate and only use dairy-free chocolate on the top layer.

Tea Cottage Scones

Tea Cottage Scones

Pre-heat oven to 200°C (425°F) Gas 7

Line several baking trays
These instructions are for making half a batch of plain and half fruit, but you can do them all one or the other. See bigger quantities listed on this and on page 17. The following quantities are based on a good sized scone, using a ruffled cutter of 7.5cm (3in)

Granulated or caster sugar can be used.

To make about 12 scones:
450g (1lb)
self raising flour

1 teaspoon salt

1 teaspoon baking powder

50g (2oz) sugar FT

75g (3oz) butter/margarine

2 eggs, beaten with warm milk about 250ml (7fl oz)

50g (2oz) sultanas/cranberries FT

zest + juice of ½ orange FT

To make about 32 big scones:
1.8 kg (4lb)
self raising flour

4 teaspoons salt

2½ teaspoons baking powder

350g (12oz) butter/margarine

225g (8oz) sugar FT

6 eggs + about 800ml (24fl oz) warmed milk

2 handfuls of sultanas/cranberries FT

zest of 1 orange, juice of ½ an orange FT

Tea Cottage Scones

🐛 Sift the self raising flour, baking powder and salt into large bowl.

🐛 Add chopped, cold butter and use a mixer on medium speed until all blended like crumbs. In a large mixer, this can take 10 minutes.

🐛 Add the sugar. Warm milk in a jug, and beat the eggs, set aside. (Add a splash of lemon or orange juice to the milk to curdle, or use a little yogurt for a richer taste.)

🐛 Zest one orange over the fruit and add the juice of half an orange, warm in microwave for 1 minute and let this infuse. (This works really well if the fruit is prepared the night before and just soaked in the juice.)

🐛 While the mixer is running with the flour and butter, add half the eggs to flour, then half of the milk, then the rest of the eggs, saving a little to paint the tops with; slowly add the rest of the warm milk until the dough is soft, pliable and not sloppy. Take out half the dough as plain and roll out very gently on a floured board. Add soaked fruit and zest to remaining dough, mix further, but don't over-mix or it chops the fruit to bits.

🐛 Gently roll out the scones, to about 5cm depth, cut with a scone cutter, being careful not to twist – just down and up with cutter! Place on paper covered trays, paint with egg/milk and bake in a hot oven until just brown and risen, about 12-14 minutes. They should not be wet or doughy, but light. Some people don't paint them with egg but just dust them with flour after.

🐛 Some recipes do not use eggs; we find the eggs help the scones stay fresh **all** day and can be adapted to any size and quantity. Watch for the number of eggs as you increase the flour/butter; it is not a straight multiplier. These scones can be frozen.

To make about
50 big scones:
**2.7kg (6lb)
self raising flour**

5 teaspoons salt

**4 teaspoons
baking powder**

**500g (18oz)
butter/margarine**

350g (12oz) sugar FT

**7 eggs, beaten plus about
1.2 litres (40fl oz
warmed milk)**

**2½ handfuls of
sultanas/cranberries FT**

**zest + juice of 1½
oranges FT**

To make about
80 scones:
**4.5kg (10lb)
self raising flour**

7 teaspoons salt

**9 teaspoons
baking powder**

**830g (1lb 14oz)
butter/ margarine**

700g (1lb 8oz) sugar FT

11 eggs, beaten

warm milk ... about
1.7 litres (60fl oz),
*(enough to make soft but
not sloppy dough)*

**3 handfuls of sultanas/
cranberries mixed**

**zest of a large
orange + juice**

(**Don't** *add juice after
soaking the fruit to the
mixture, as it can make
it too sloppy and gooey)*

Some thoughts on scones ...

🐦 We always use free range eggs and mostly organic flour, Fairtrade fruit and sugar. Sometimes we add a little Fairtrade cinnamon to the mix. We make ours with white unbleached flour, but there are good wholemeal recipes around, see Delia Smith.

🐦 Always use a 'light touch' with scones – don't handle them too much, or bash them like bread dough. Be gentle. Keep them rising and soft.

🐦 The traditional way to serve scones is with clotted cream (we prefer Rodda's from Cornwall) and jam.

A note on our jam: *we cannot make enough to supply the constant demand, so we mix some very high grade organic high fruit jam with* *the nicest brand of bulk strawberry jam from a local supplier.*

There, the secret's out. If guests want butter we will offer it, but does **anyone** really need both butter and clotted cream? (My husband says **yes!** But then he doesn't like jam ...)

Dairy-Free:
Can these be made dairy-free? Yes, use non-dairy margarine instead of butter and an alternative milk such as rice, hemp or soya and omit the clotted cream. Sigh.

Date and Oat Scones

Makes 6–8 scones

Preheat oven to 220°C
(425°F) Gas 7

Lightly grease, spray with
oil or line a baking sheet

175g (6oz)
self raising flour

1 teaspoon
baking powder

2 teaspoons ground
cinnamon FT

50g (2oz)
butter/margarine

50g (2oz) caster sugar FT

75g (3oz) chopped
dried dates FT

125g (5oz) porridge oats

150ml (6fl oz)
natural yogurt

1 free range egg, beaten

Date and Oat Scones

🍂 Sift the flour, baking powder and cinnamon into a bowl and rub in the butter until the mixture resembles breadcrumbs.

🍂 Stir in the sugar, dates and oats.

🍂 Beat the yogurt and egg together, and add to the bowl and mix to form a soft dough. Add a tablespoon of milk, or two, if too dry.

🍂 Tip the dough onto a floured surface and knead lightly. Press the dough out gently to form a 23cm (9.5in) circle (lunch plate), mark 6 or 8 wedges.

🍂 Place on a baking sheet and bake for 10–15 minutes until well risen and golden brown. Serve warm with honey and clotted cream, which is a pleasant change from the traditional cream and jam thing. They can be cut as traditional scones with a round cutter, but making them wedges of a circle adds variety to the display.

🍂 These freeze well, especially if you are going to reheat in the microwave, heat only for a few seconds and serve.

Cheese Scones

Makes about 10

Preheat oven to 220°C (400°F) Gas 7

Spray a baking tray with oil or line with parchment
Scone cutter

175g (6oz) self raising flour

½ teaspoon salt

½ teaspoon dry mustard or 1 teaspoon mustard

25g (1oz) butter/margarine

75-150g (3-5 oz) grated strong cheddar cheese or similar

(Former Tea Cottage Team member Lea says you can't add too much cheese!)

1 free range egg, beaten

2-2½ tablespoons milk

a couple of good pinches of cayenne pepper and a little extra milk

Cheese Scones

🌿 Measure the flour and all dry ingredients, then rub in the butter and most of the cheese.

🌿 Beat the egg and milk together and add to make a smooth dough.

🌿 Roll out to 3cm depth and cut with a round cutter. Any size is fine. Cut cleanly without twisting, just bring the cutter straight up. Place on a lined baking sheet. Brush with the remaining milk and sprinkle the remaining cheese and a dash of pepper on each one.

🌿 Bake for 15–20 minutes and serve warm.

🌿 These freeze well. This recipe also can be doubled or quadrupled, it still works very well. We serve cheese scones with crème fraîche and homemade chutney or apple butter.

🌿 You can add other herbs/spices, or sun dried tomatoes, or how about chopped, stoned Fairtrade olives? If you make tiny scones, cut them open and spread with cream cheese, chives, or chutney, or olives and use as canapés for those important gatherings!

🌿 Try using a mixture of sharp cheddar and parmesan, or take this opportunity to use up random bits of cheese from the fridge. Any cheese still safe could go into Bird Cakes, see page 31.

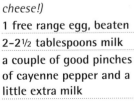

Cathy's Carrot Cake with Mascarpone Icing

Preheat oven to 180°C (350°F) Gas 4

Spray with oil and line 2 x 23cm (9in) cake tins

3 x free range eggs, separated

250g (9oz) self raising flour

½ teaspoon bicarbonate of soda

1 teaspoon baking powder

1½ teaspoons cinnamon FT

pinch of salt

200 ml (6½fl oz) sunflower oil

250g (9oz) light brown sugar FT

150g (5oz) carrots, washed and grated

juice of ½ a lemon FT

150g (5oz) chopped walnuts FT

For the Icing:
250g (9oz) mascarpone cheese

200g (7oz) cream cheese

150g (5oz) icing sugar FT

5 drops orange oil

a handful of walnut halves FT

*This moist cake keeps well for a day or two, and can be frozen **before** you ice it (defrost partly, then ice and let it continue to defrost and keep the creamy topping cool.) It could also be made in muffin tins, lined with papers; bake them for about 30+ minutes and watch for them to be well risen and bounce back when nudged.*

Cathy's Carrot Cake with Mascarpone Icing

Cathy Park is leading the Tea Cottage Team in 2013 and this cake will no doubt go on to be be a firm favourite. Some people even say that Carrot Cake counts as one of your five vegetables for the day!

🌱 Sift together the flour, bicarbonate of soda, baking powder, cinnamon and salt and set aside.

🌱 Beat the oil and sugar in a mixer until well creamed, then add the yolks one at a time, mixing well after each one. Add the grated carrots, the lemon juice and the walnuts.

🌱 Fold in the flour mixture using a a slow setting in a mixer, or if by hand, gently with a metal spoon – not beating it.

🌱 Now, beat the egg whites in a clean, oil free bowl until stiff peaks form. Gently fold this into the mixture with a metal spoon. Divide the mixture between the two tins and bake in the centre of the oven for 40–45 minutes, testing with a skewer to see if it is done. The skewer should come out clean.

🌱 Cool in the tins for 10 minutes, then carefully turn out and cool completely on a wire rack.

For the icing:
Mix the cheeses and sugar together until thick and smooth; add the orange oil. When the cakes are cooled, sandwich them together with the icing and then cover the top layer and the sides if you have enough. Top with walnut halves and enjoy!

Tea Cottage 🍎 Lee Abbey Devon

A note about eggs:
Debbie, a friend from Brighton says she weighs her eggs first; so if she were doing this recipe, she would weigh as close to 400g of cracked open eggs and then use that measurement for the sugar, flour and fat. That way if the eggs are especially smaller or larger than last time, she gets it all equal. This could be very helpful for the larger cake, as it makes it more accurate. Which should make the cake consistently turn out its best and that is a wonderful idea.
Go Debbie!

**Tea Cottage Cakes,
two layers each**

Makes 14 generous slices

**Preheat oven to 180°C
(350°F) Gas 4**

**Spray with oil and line
with baking parchment
2 x 23cm (9in) tins**

**The basic
ingredients are:
400g (14oz)
butter or margarine**

**400g (14oz)
caster sugar FT**

**7 free range eggs,
lightly beaten**

**400g (14oz)
self raising flour**

**2½ teaspoons
baking powder**

*These cakes last for about
4 days if covered; they
taste their best in the first
2 days. They can be frozen
if wrapped well, before
being decorated.*

*Dairy-Free
If you use dairy-free
margarine and not lemon
curd, they are 'dairy-free'
cakes, so the
Victoria Sponge could
have rose water icing and
jam instead of cream.*

Tea Cottage Cakes
two layers each

Start by beating the fat and sugar until really fluffy; measure the flour and baking powder and sift onto a large piece of baking parchment (use afterwards to line the two tins).

Beat the eggs very well; then add the flour and eggs alternately and blend well after each addition. Scrape the bowl and add the extra bits. Bake for about 20-24 minutes.

Coffee and Walnut

Add ½ cup of chopped walnuts and 3 tablespoons espresso or strong coffee. When baked, drizzle a little coffee over the cakes while still warm. Make coffee icing by mixing margarine and icing sugar, then add 1-2 tablespoons strong coffee. Sprinkle chopped walnuts and walnut halves between layers and especially on top. You can get them Fairtrade.

Lemon Drizzle

Add the zest of one lemon to the cake mixture and the juice of half the lemon at the end.

When baked, drizzle a little juice over the cakes while still warm. Then sandwich together with good quality lemon curd and top with a thin lemon juice and icing sugar glaze; decorate with tiny pieces of lemon or zest. (See Delia Smith for making your own very high quality Lemon Curd.)

Victoria Sponge

For a Victoria Sponge Cake, add to the basic ingredients 1½ teaspoons vanilla FT.

When baked, sandwich together with strawberry jam and whipped cream and dust the top layer with icing sugar. A very nice alternative is to replace the vanilla with **rose** water and use this in a frosting made of margarine and icing sugar.

Shortbread Millionaires or Chocolate Caramel Shortbread

Shortbread Millionaires or Chocolate Caramel Shortbread

Preheat oven 150°C (300°F) Gas 2

Line baking tin approximately 25 x 30cm (10 x 12in)

Base:
225g (8oz) plain flour
100g (4oz) caster sugar FT
225g (8oz) butter
100g (4oz) ground almonds or ground rice

Caramel:
175g (6oz) butter
175g (6oz) caster sugar FT
4 tablespoons golden syrup FT
397g can condensed milk

Top layer:
200g (8oz) dark chocolate FT
30g butter (1½oz) (optional)

Thus named by a Team member for whom English was a third language, but it gave connotations of someone gaining such earthly wealth from shortbread.
What a nice idea ...

Base:
❦ Mix the butter and sugar together until well blended, then add the ground rice or almonds and flour. Mix all until smooth, then press into the tin. Prick all over with a fork, and bake 15–18 minutes or until just lightly going brown. Remove and cool on a rack whilst making the caramel layer.

Caramel:
❦ Put all the ingredients in a saucepan and stir over a low heat until the butter dissolves; bubble the mixture for 5–8 minutes stirring constantly until thick and fudge-like. (The caramel **wants** to burn on to the pan – stir it constantly!) Pour over the base and let it cool.

Top layer:
❦ When cool, melt 200g Fairtrade dark chocolate over hot water (not boiling) and spread over the caramel. For an even richer version, former Tea Cottage worker Julianna found adding some butter to the chocolate layer did the trick!

See page 71 for how to save and use ingredients that didn't get burnt and deal with burnt pans.

Cathy Park's Grandma's Devon Apple Cake

Preheat oven to 170°C (325°F) Gas 3

Spray with oil and line a 25cm (10in) square tin

225g (8oz) cooking apples, peeled, cored and chopped

110g (4oz) sultanas FT and enough cider to just cover – soak overnight

150ml (5fl oz) milk

175g (6oz) soft brown sugar FT

350g (12oz) self raising flour

2 teaspoons mixed spice

175g (6oz) margarine

1 free range egg, beaten

25g (1oz) demerara sugar FT

Soak sultanas in cider overnight.

Cathy Park's Grandma's Devon Apple Cake

Cathy's Grandma lived in Topsham in south Devon and as someone in the family couldn't pronounce her real name – Nellie – she was known as Moley! She always baked this special cake for the family and Cathy is kindly sharing it with us. What genius to soak the fruit in cider. It sounds yummy from the off!

In a bowl mix the apples, sultanas, milk, soft brown sugar and mixed spice together. Rub the margarine into the flour.

Add the fruit mixture and egg to the flour mixture and mix well.

Spread into the prepared tin and sprinkle the demerara sugar over the top.

Bake for 1½ hours. The cake is done when it is well risen and bounces back when pressed in the centre.

This cake would be delicious with clotted cream and maybe the rest of the bottle of cider? Thank you Cathy and Grandma Moley.

Pixie Dust

organic golden
caster sugar FT

ground vanilla pod FT

ground cinnamon FT
– lots!

50g (2oz) per 500g (1lb)
sugar or more

ground ginger FT – add
less than the other spices

a few whole cloves FT left
in jar to infuse

Pixie Dust
Never published before secret recipe!

🐝 Mix all the ingredients together.

🐝 Scrape out the seeds from a vanilla pod and chop and crush with some sugar (maybe 1 pod to 500g (1lb) sugar).

🐝 Store in a sealed jar and stir occasionally and then pour into shakers.

In 2007, my husband David and I had the privilege of visiting the beautiful island country of Sri Lanka. Through the kind help of Steenbergs Spices and friends, we were able to meet some Fairtrade growers from the Sri Lanka Organic Farmers Association – SOFA. They showed us with such pride the beautiful spices and tea they grew and all the self and community-empowering things they did with their Fairtrade premiums. I was hooked!

Here is a little something to show our solidarity with these people and farmers all over the world who grow our food. Enjoy!

This makes a wonderful gift for anyone except diabetics, especially if you find some vintage or antique sugar shakers to fill with *Pixie Dust*. Or buy it at Lee Abbey, Devon.

Lea's German Apple Cake

Serves 12-14

Preheat oven 200°C (400°F) Gas 6

Lightly spray a loose bottom 23cm (9in) round cake tin with oil

Base:

3 egg whites and 2 tablespoons warm water

3 egg yolks

75g (3oz) caster sugar FT

2 teaspoons baking powder

75g (3oz) plain flour

2 tablespoons custard powder (such as Bird's, not the instant type)

Top Layer:

500ml (18fl oz) apple juice FT

3 tablespoons lemon juice and 2 tablespoons water

2 eggs

160g (5½oz) caster sugar FT

5 tablespoons custard powder (such as Bird's, not the instant type)

5 to 6 apples peeled, cored and grated

1½ tablespoons cinnamon FT

50g (2oz) butter

Lea's German Apple Cake

Former Tea Cottage Team member Lea taught us this interesting variation on apple cake the year we had plenty of apples growing just alongside the Tea Cottage.
Light and delicious, it suits a summer garden party or barbecue.

🍵 Mix together the egg yolks, sugar, baking powder, plain flour and custard powder – you may need to add some milk if it's too thick. **Fold in the whisked egg whites/water** last. Spread in the tin and bake for 12 minutes. Leave to cool in the tin.

🍵 Cook all the top layer ingredients in a saucepan, adding the butter when it is simmering and keep stirring until thick and custard-like. Pour on to the cooled base and chill in the fridge overnight to set.

🍵 Serve with pouring cream. A cool, summery cake that could be decorated with piped whip cream and glacé ginger.

Pixie's Little Cinnamon Buns

Preheat oven 200°C (400°F) Gas 6

Spray two large cake tins or small roasting tins with oil

Dough:
600g (1lb 5oz) organic **strong** white flour

2 teaspoons fast acting yeast (the type you add to the flour) usually one sachet

½ teaspoon salt

1 tablespoon caster sugar FT

about 270 ml (10fl oz) warm water/milk mixture

25g (1oz) butter/margarine

1 free range egg

Filling:
150g (5oz) butter, mix until softened

75g (3oz) soft brown sugar FT

3 teaspoons cinnamon FT

75g (3oz) sultanas, raisins, currants chopped

40g (1½oz) chopped nuts (optional) Pecans are best

½ teaspoon vanilla essence FT

zest of an orange is nice to add too

Drizzle Topping:
icing sugar FT

orange or lemon juice FT

Pixie's Little Cinnamon Buns

🐦 Sift the flour, salt and sugar into a bowl and stir in the yeast. Make a well and add some of the water/milk and draw together the dough and add more liquid until a nice pliable dough is formed.

🐦 Add the egg and smoosh it in, adding a little more flour if needed to not make a sticky mess.

🐦 Put onto a floured surface and knead it for about 8 minutes, or use a dough hook in a big mixer bowl. Wash the bowl out and drizzle a little oil around it. Then use the dough to spread the oil and end upside down with oil over the top. Or use butter.

🐦 Cover with a tea towel, place somewhere warm and leave to double. This might take an hour, or probably less.

🐦 Punch down the dough (oooh, I love this bit!) and gently knead it until even and smooth.

To make up the filling:
🐦 Mix all the filling ingredients with the softened butter.

🐦 Roll the dough out into a large rectangle, maybe 15 x 50cm (6 x 20in).

🐦 Spread the filling over all the dough, except leave a border clear around the edges. Roll up the dough along the **long** side, squeezing and pinching it closed when finished. Cut the long fat snake of goodness into 1 inch slices, placing them as circles fairly near each other in the tins. Cover loosely with tea towels and leave to rise again (like we will one day). Bake for 12–15 minutes until golden brown.

❦ Take them out of the oven and cool slightly.

❦ Then make up a drizzle of icing sugar FT mixed with orange or lemon juice, fairly thin and drizzly. If you want it to show up white and distinctive, wait until the rolls are cooled and make the icing a little thicker.

❦ Eaten warm, they are divine. These freeze really well and can be reheated in the microwave. Serve with butter if you must! These **can** be made dairy-free with good margarine in place of butter and just water in the dough instead of water/milk mixture.

Note: *The closer you set them in the tin to bake, the more they keep their shape, however if they are too close they may not cook through. Just keep an eye on them.*

Inger's Celebration Cake (Gluten-Free)

Serves about 10

Preheat oven to 170°C (325°F) Gas 3

Lightly grease and line a 23cm (9in) cake tin, ideally loose bottom

4 egg whites free range

300g (11oz) caster sugar FT

350g (12oz) ground almonds

Caramelized egg custard topping:

4 egg yolks, free range

100g (4oz) caster sugar FT

100g (4oz) butter

1½ teaspoon vanilla essence FT

double cream – about 125ml (5fl oz) but a mixture of milk and cream will work if you don't have enough

Inger's Celebration Cake
(Gluten-Free)

This cake was very popular when Inger Denniston, who is originally from Norway, led the Tea Cottage. The Team decorated the Celebration Cake with strawberries, raspberries and blueberries in the form of a Union Jack. Extremely delicious and of course gluten-free.

🍎 Whisk egg whites to stiff peak stage; add sugar a small amount at a time; carefully fold in ground almonds with a slotted spoon. Don't bang or jar.

🍎 Spread in the cake tin and bake for about 45 minutes until slightly brown and set. Cool whilst making the topping.

Topping:

🍎 Mix all but yolks in pan and stir vigorously; boil together until it thickens, don't let it burn!

🍎 Remove and add yolks, return to heat until almost boiling; stir lots, then cool slightly as it sets and gets a skin if left too long. Pour over the cake and decorate with fruit as per the occasion.

🍎 This can be frozen before pouring on the topping, the topping can be frozen in a zip-lock bag or small box. Defrost slowly and proceed to decorate.

Bird Cakes

Left over:

bread

toast

crackers

apple/pear cores

seeds/nuts

fat

Bird Cakes

These are for the birds, not cooked with birds! The discussion will rage about whether or not we should put out food for birds, but if you agree we should, here is a good way to use up those little scraps from your kitchen.
Keep the cakes up in nets, away from potential rodents, including squirrels ...

❦ Gather leftover bits of bread crumbs, toast scraps, crackers, ends of cheese, fruit cake and apple/pear cores and peel; chop them up really small. Add any seeds/nuts (being careful to always chop peanuts really small) and dried fruit.

❦ Melt lard and any edges of fat from cooking bacon or ham. Pour fat over the dry goodies; mix and either form into balls to fit into small nets left from other packaging, or into moulds like muffin tins or yogurt pots. It works best if you put them to chill, so the fat sets hard.

❦ Then either string them up into trees, or hang below a bird table.

❦ Great use of those scones you burnt but don't want to admit to! – stale bread ends etc. and maybe a few specially purchased garden bird seeds also boost the nutrients for our feathered friends.

❦ Sue Redbond, past Community member, packs all the ingredients into large pine cones and hangs them by a wire from branches.

❦ We make these at the Tea Cottage. The birds love them! Now we need to train the birds **not** to pinch the homemade fudge from the guests' saucers.

Seriously Rich Chocolate Cake (Gluten-Free)

Serves 6-8
Preheat over to 170°C (325°F) Gas 3
Spray with oil and line the base of a loose bottom 20 cm (8in) cake tin

100g (4oz) butter (see note on page 33)
140g (5oz) dark chocolate FT at least 60% cocoa solids
6 free range eggs, separated
pinch of salt
140g (5oz) ground almonds
1 teaspoon vanilla essence FT
85g (3oz) caster sugar FT
cocoa powder FT for dusting
crème fraîche (can be half-fat variety)
seasonal fruit and coulis FT to serve

Fairtrade Coulis:
100ml (3.5fl oz) fruit puree
3 teaspoons caster sugar FT
a few drops of water

See page 75 for suppliers of fruit puree.

Seriously Rich Chocolate Cake
(Gluten-Free)

This always gets rave reviews, particularly from the folk who are on a gluten-free diet and often have few options at cake time.

🍃 Melt the butter and chocolate, stir until smooth; leave for about 5 minutes to cool slightly. Stir in the egg yolks, ground almonds and vanilla.

🍃 Put the egg whites into a clean grease-free bowl, add a pinch of salt and whisk until soft peaks form. Continue whisking, sprinkling in sugar a little at a time, until stiff peaks form. Stir 2 tablespoons of the whites into the chocolate mixture. Carefully fold in the remainder of the whites.

🍃 Spoon the mixture into the prepared tin and bake for 30-35 minutes until well risen and just firm. Cool in the tin. Remove the cake and peel away the paper. Dust with cocoa powder.

🍃 The **cake can be frozen at this point** for up to 3 weeks. Place in a freezer container with space around the cake, as it is easily dented.

🍃 Serve with crème fraîche, fruit coulis or syrup, fruit and clotted cream and a little sprinkle of *Pixie Dust*.

🍃 **Fairtrade Coulis:**
Mix 100ml fruit puree with 3 teaspoons Fairtrade caster sugar, heat until the sugar dissolves. Depending on fruit type, add a little more sugar and if needed, a few drops of water; simmer until it reduces to a good pouring consistency. Drizzle across a plate; place a slice of cake on the top, pile seasonal fruit alongside, a good blob of cream and a dusting of *Pixie Dust*!

*This recipe does
work with good
quality margarine,
however butter
tastes better!
If you require
dairy-free, use
non-dairy margarine
and chocolate
and serve without
the cream.*

Lee Abbey Apple and Almond Cake

Serves 8-10

Preheat oven to 160°C (325°F) Gas 3

Spray and line a 20 or 22cm (8 or 9in) round tin; loose bottom is good

175g (6oz) softened butter

175g (6oz) caster sugar FT

1 teaspoon vanilla essence FT

3 free range eggs, lightly beaten

50g (2oz) ground almonds

grated zest and juice of ½ orange/lemon FT

100g (4oz) plain flour, sifted

100g (4oz) self raising flour, sifted

2 tablespoons milk

200g (8oz) chunks of peeled, cored apples (any type of apple or a mixture of several types) – chop them into juice and zest

2½ teaspoons cinnamon FT

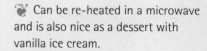

Lee Abbey Apple and Almond Cake

❧ Cream the butter and sugar, add vanilla and eggs, and add the almonds. Fold in sifted flours, cinnamon and milk, then add apples and juice/zest.

❧ Put the mixture in the cake tin. Bake for about 40-60 minutes. Serve warm with clotted cream, dusted with *Pixie Dust*.

❧ Can be re-heated in a microwave and is also nice as a dessert with vanilla ice cream.

❧ **This Apple Cake freezes** well and can be made tall and thick or wider and thinner. Check timings for baking, as the 8 inch tin will take longer to cook right through. Wrap in baking parchment and then a sealed container or foil for the freezer.

❧ This recipe can be doubled. It could be made dairy-free with good margarine instead of butter and more fruit juice instead of milk. It is nice with half pears/half apple and ginger for zing!

This cake is seriously amazing, just probably the most calories per bite ever ... Sigh!

Lucie's Chocolate Guinness Cake

Serves 12-14

Preheat oven 180°C (350°F) Gas 4

Spray a 23cm (9in) tin with oil and line the base with baking parchment

250ml (9fl oz) Guinness

250g (9oz) butter

75g (3oz) cocoa FT

400g (14oz) caster sugar FT

142g (5oz) crème fraîche or a mixture of full cream yogurt and clotted cream

2 eggs, beaten with crème fraîche/yogurt

1 tablespoon vanilla FT

275g (10oz) plain flour

2½ teaspoons bicarbonate of soda

Topping:

400g (14oz) cream cheese

200g (7oz) icing sugar FT

170ml (6fl oz) double or whipping cream or 60-85g (2-3oz) single cream and 85g (3oz) clotted cream beaten together

Lucie's Chocolate Guinness Cake

🍏 Pour Guinness into a large saucepan, add the butter cut into slices and heat until the butter melts. Remove pan from heat; whisk in the cocoa and sugar.

🍏 Beat the cream/yogurt with the eggs and vanilla, pour into the saucepan and finally sift the flour with the bicarbonate of soda and stir into the chocolate mixture.

🍏 Pour into the prepared tin and bake for 45-60 minutes. The cake is done when it begins to draw away from the sides and bounces back when very gently pushed in the middle. Leave the cake to cool in the tin, remove to a rack.

Topping:

🍏 Lightly whip the cream cheese until smooth. Sieve over the icing sugar and beat both together. Add the cream and beat until thick and spreadable. When the cake is cool, ice the top to resemble the froth on the top of a pint.

🍏 This cake is really moist and delicious on its own, or served with raspberries, strawberries and/or blueberries. It is also nice warm, served with the icing on the side to melt in.

Thank you Lucie Mitton, another lovely former Tea Cottage Team member.

Peanut Butter Chocolate Chip Cookies

Makes about 40 depending on size

Preheat oven 180°C (350°F) Gas 4

Spray with oil or line a baking tray

300g (10oz) plain flour

1 teaspoon bicarbonate of soda

1 teaspoon salt

200g (8oz) margarine

150g (6oz) soft dark brown sugar FT

150g (6oz) granulated or caster sugar FT

2 free range eggs

1 teaspoon vanilla essence FT

325g (12oz) crunchy peanut butter FT

100g (4oz) dark chocolate FT, chopped into small chunks or chocolate chips

Peanut Butter Chocolate Chip Cookies

🐦 Cream the margarine and both sugars until soft and fluffy. Lightly mix the egg and vanilla; gradually mix into margarine/sugar. Stir in the peanut butter.

🐦 Sift the flour and bicarbonate of soda and stir into the mixture. Add the chunks of chocolate. Chill the dough for 1 hour if you can to make it easier to handle.

🐦 Now spoon rounded teaspoons of the dough onto baking sheets; press down if chilled. Bake for about 12–15 minutes and cool on a rack.

Variations: if you only have half a jar of peanut butter, it will still work. But the more peanut butter the richer and 'shorter' the batter. You can replace half the flour with wholemeal plain flour for an even more nutty and nutritious choice. Or replace two tablespoons of plain flour with oatmeal for more texture and a thicker cookie.

These keep in a tin for about one week, but at our house they last about an hour! For dairy-free, use dairy-free margarine and chocolate chopped into small chunks.

Lee Abbey Tea Cottage Garden Lavender Shortbread

Makes approximately 20 depending on size

Preheat oven to 190°C (375°F) Gas 5

Spray with oil or line baking trays with baking parchment

250g (9oz)
caster sugar FT

9 dried lavender flowers, unsprayed, removed from stalks

450g (1lb)
softened butter

450g (1lb) plain flour

240g (8oz) ground rice

½ teaspoon salt

extra caster sugar
and lavender flowers
to decorate

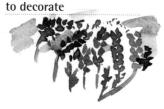

Lee Abbey Tea Cottage Garden Lavender Shortbread

🍂 Put half the sugar and the lavender flowers in a food processor and blitz for 10 seconds. If you don't have one, use a mortar and pestle to crush small and mix the flowers with several spoonfuls of sugar.

🍂 Blend with the rest of the sugar and then cream with the butter until pale and fluffy. Stir in the flour, rice and salt until like fine crumbs, then with your hands, smoosh it all together and knead for a few minutes. Put into a clean plastic bag or cling film and place into the fridge for 30 minutes to firm up.

🍂 Press out the dough gently and

cut into small squares, about 5mm (¼ in) thick, vary in size (so you can stack them when cooked and cooled). Place on trays and bake for 15–20 minutes until pale golden. Yum!

🍂 Sprinkle straight away with a little caster sugar and leave to cool on the trays for about 10 minutes. Then cool completely on wire racks and serve with extra lavender flowers.

They look the business when tied up with lavender coloured ribbon and a tiny bunch of flowers. Sweet! These will keep about a week in a tin, but just eat them. Give them away and enjoy the scent of summer gardens.

Note: *Save the stems of the lavender flowers, tie with string or raffia, dip in melted candle ends and use as fire starters in a fireplace or beach fire or barbeque. These make nice gifts too.*

Lee Abbey Firelighters

dry twigs/pine cones

dried seed pods

out-of-date spices

scented oils

old potpourri

old candle ends

Lee Abbey Firelighters

We often make these as part of an afternoon workshop and they are great fun. We use the cheapest muffin papers and some old muffin tins which we line.

Gather little dry twigs, leaves, pine cones, teasels, nut shells and very dry mosses and any old bits of potpourri or the like. Sprinkle them around in the muffin papers and top them with a little bit of out-of-date spices or scented oils.

Carefully melt old candle ends and pour them over the bits in the papers. Let them set completely and when cooled, keep them in a basket by the fire to help get the kindling really going.

You can use old wicks from candles as well, but you don't need them as you just need to light the edge of the muffin papers. These make a nice gift for anyone with an open fire or wood burner and they also work in barbeques or for a beach fire.

On a recent visit to Iona Abbey in Scotland, I noted that they make firelighters as thin slabs of melted wax with twigs in them and sell them as two bars/slabs, tied together and with instructions to crumble them on the fire. Nice!

Fair Banana Nut Bread

Preheat oven 180°C (350°F) Gas 4

Spray 2 x 1lb loaf tins with oil and line the bottom of the tins or line muffin tins with paper liners

450g (1lb) plain flour

6 teaspoons baking powder

2 teaspoons salt

1 teaspoon cinnamon FT

½ teaspoon ground nutmeg FT

200g (7oz) butter or margarine

300g (11oz) soft light brown sugar FT

4 free range eggs

5-6 well ripened bananas* FT

110g (4oz) chopped walnuts/pecans/hazelnuts FT (optional)

Fair Banana Nut Bread

🍎 Sift all dry ingredients and set aside. Cream the butter/margarine and sugar together until light and fluffy.

🍎 Lightly whisk the eggs, add the mashed bananas and beat into the creamed mixture, a little at a time. Sift the dry ingredients again over the creamed mixture and fold together gently.

🍎 Lastly, fold in the chopped nuts, if you are using them.

🍎 Pour the mixture into the tins, or scoop into muffin papers and bake for 1 hour for loaves, or 30-35 minutes for larger muffins. They are done when they are well risen and bounce back when gently touched on top.

🍎 Cool in the tins and then on a rack.

🍎 This recipe is even better if left for 24 hours after baking. When completely cooled, wrap the loaves in baking parchment, then in a tin or foil. Serve sliced with butter, or for muffins, with butter or a small amount of clotted cream. If making dairy-free, serve with good margarine. This freezes very well and is the perfect present for new neighbours or someone just back from being away.

Bananas were one of the earliest products to carry the Fairtrade mark. Through the work of the Fairtrade Foundation and many others, the lives of banana farmers and their communities are now thriving and flourishing. Whole islands have been saved from near slavery and economic and environmental exploitation. **Keep buying Fairtrade – it really does make a difference.**

*Bananas can be frozen! Especially when you have a glut of really ripe ones. Peel them and freeze in zip-lock bags and use for bread or smoothies! They generate a lot of liquid which makes the bread/ muffins even more deliciously moist. For smoothies, use straight from the freezer; for bread/muffins defrost and use with liquid.

Réka's Mum's Hungarian Cake

Preheat oven to 180°C (350°F) Gas 4, then later down to 150°C (300°F)

Spray with oil and line a 23–27cm (9–10in) square cake tin

250g (9oz) plain flour

125g (4½oz) margarine

50g (2oz) caster sugar FT

1 egg

50ml (2fl oz) sour cream or cream cheese and natural yogurt

1 teaspoon yeast – the dried type you add directly to the flour

For between layers:
most of a jar of good apricot jam

60g (2½oz) ground walnuts FT

60g (2½oz) caster sugar FT, ground and mixed with walnuts

For top:
100g (3½oz) dark chocolate FT

25g (scant 1oz) margarine

Réka's Mum's Hungarian Cake

A former Tea Cottage Team member, Réka Szentjobi who met her true love at Lee Abbey, gave us this interesting Hungarian Cake recipe and taught us how to prepare it. The cake is made of thin layers of sweet yeast bread, stacked with apricot jam and ground walnuts and topped with chocolate. Be the first in your circle to turn up with something new for the next shared meal!

❧ Mix all the first list of ingredients together to make a nice dough. Divide the dough into four and roll out each piece to a thin, flat layer the size of your cake tin.

❧ Now place the first flat layer in the tin, top with apricot jam and a sprinkling of the walnuts/sugar. Repeat with other layers, ending with just a dough layer on top.

❧ Bake in a hot oven for 5 minutes, then turn the oven down to 150°C (300°F) Gas 2 for about 35-40 minutes, until lightly brown and risen slightly.

❧ Cool in the tin, setting it on a rack. When completely cool, melt chocolate and margarine over simmering hot water and spread on the top of the cake. Cut into small pieces and enjoy a little of Eastern Europe via Lee Abbey.

Note: *If you line the tin with enough paper to come up the sides, it helps to be able to lift the cake out, rather than have to turn it over!*

W.H. Bailey.   Lady Smith.   Mrs Bailey.   Charles E. Wilde.
Mr H. Pollock.   Mrs H. Pollock.   Mr Phippen.

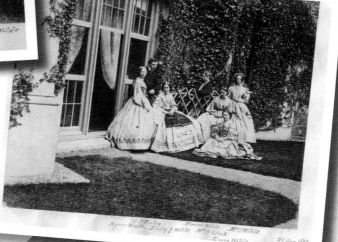

C. H. Bailey.   Francis Wilde.   Mrs Wilde.
Agnes Wilde.   Emily J. Wilde.   Mrs H. Pollock.
Louisa Wilde.   22 Aug. 1863.

Photographs above and right, taken in 1863 picturing members of the Bailey family and friends

Above right, the view towards Lee Bay has remained unchanged, as shown by the recent photographs on pages 47 and 48

History of Lee Abbey

LEE ABBEY IS IN FACT NOT an Abbey! It is, however, the home of an international Christian Community, who number about 100 folk of all ages, who live, work and pray together, serving the guests that come to the Christian Conference, Retreat and Holiday Centre and The Beacon Activity Centre. But it has not always been like this ...

In the ninth century, the farmland was owned by an order of monks from Dorset and although the brothers never established a monastery here, it was a part of their holdings and run to support their work. After the dissolution of the monasteries, it came into private hands and was a working farm with a large farmhouse. Some of the flagstones and a decorative wall portion still remain today.

Later, that building was demolished and when a gentleman known as Squire Bailey bought the property, he built a grander affair, using his work as a land agent to acquire the Octagonal Lounge windows and the substantial Green Staircase. He was very adept as one of the early photographers and many excellent images from his life at Lee Abbey remain in the archives. It was Squire Bailey who renamed the location 'Lee Abbey' and even built the Tower Lodge

as a folly, to give the name credence. His son died without an heir and the land was sold to a hotelier. The hotel had a golf course, and the early days of motoring holidays encouraged visitors to between-the-wars houseparties.

During WWII a Sussex school was evacuated to Lee Abbey. In 1945, six Christian men of vision and faith, some of whom had run evangelistic houseparties at Lee Abbey in the 1943–44 summer holidays, backed by much prayer, purchased the house and estate as a centre for evangelism. Early discussions of this great venture of faith took place over a cup of coffee in the Tea Cottage! The men and women called by God to serve at Lee Abbey became a community whose international nature radically challenged post-war prejudices as young people from Germany, France, Holland and Britain worked alongside each other. The Community has grown over the years, united by a common desire to share the love of Christ with whoever comes to us and to renew and serve the church.

Today that vision of 'communicating Christ through relationships' continues, as it is outworked through the life of the Community; through the conferences, retreats and holidays on offer and the summer camps; and through teams going out to work alongside churches around the country, to share the love of God with their neighbours.

In the 1960's a similar Community to that in Devon was established in London, where they provide a 'home from home' for hundreds of international students. Small Missional Communities which are all part of the Lee Abbey Movement, are in Aston in Birmingham, Knowle West in Bristol and Acton Vale in London. These Communities live, work and pray together, sharing what God has given them with their local area.

A growing number of Lee Abbey Friends of Jesus provide crucial prayer support for all areas of the Movement. Groups of Friends gather all over the UK, and in several countries around the world, for fellowship and to stand alongside the work of Lee Abbey. God has been very faithful since 1946. Many thousands of Community and guests have experienced Lee Abbey, a special place based on our amazing God, living and working to his praise and glory.

For more details about Lee Abbey Devon, please see our website: **www.leeabbey.org.uk/devon** or write to us at: Lee Abbey Lynton Devon EX35 6JJ England.

History of The Tea Cottage at Lee Abbey Devon

THE TEA COTTAGE AT LEE ABBEY has been operating for over 65 years. It was previously run by Mrs. Budd from the Lee Cottage kitchen. She was assisted by Ursula Kay, who was also a very accomplished nature artist and keen student of all that grew and lived on God's earth!

Ursula helped lead the Estate Team, as well as running the Tea Cottage in the summer. She wrote a truly delightful book called *'He gave us eyes to see them'*, which she richly illustrated with her own drawings. In it she records each new bird's arrival in spring, the nests, progress of hatchlings and alongside that, the weather patterns, growth of many species of plants and trees and the movement of mammals across the estate and woods nearby. She also recollected the day when the Team at the Tea Cottage served 300 cream teas plus cakes and ice creams! That put the fear of God into this Community member starting out leading the Tea Cottage!

After her untimely death, during John and Gay Perry's leadership of the Devon Community, she gave the Tea Cottage and Lee Cottage to Lee Abbey. Since then it has been run by various Community members, supplemented by a few volunteers, summer workers

Miss Delbridge's Tea Gardens, Lee Bay, Lynton

Prayer Box
Please feel free to place any prayer requests in the Tea Caddy; we meet to pray as a Team each morning.

and much heavenly support! Each morning during the season, the Tea Cottage Team gather to taste the fresh scones and pray for the day. Guests have always been offered the chance to put prayer requests to the Team. These needs are lifted to the Heavenly Father,

LEE ABBEY FROM THE WEST, LYNTON.

who knows us all better than we know ourselves. Many answers to prayer have been noted and many are known only to those involved. God has been faithful and his blessings outnumber even the scones served in 65 years!

Tea Cottage 🍎 Lee Abbey Devon

Savoury Delights

Tea Cottage
Apple Butter

180°C (350°F) Gas 4

Large preserving or stock pan plus a large, deep roasting tin

Makes several jars. Thoroughly wash jam or other jars, with well fitting lids that have an intact coated surface inside the lids. Place them on an oven tray to sterilise when needed.*

1 litre (35fl oz) of apple sauce

410g (14oz) caster sugar FT, white or soft brown

60ml (3fl oz) cider vinegar

1-2 teaspoons cinnamon or more

¼ teaspoon ground cloves

Label and date; apple butter will keep for at least 8 months in a cool, dark place. Make nice labels and give as gifts, perhaps with a dozen cheese scones! Once opened, keep in the fridge.

Tea Cottage Apple Butter, Dairy-Free

This is a very old American recipe from the Mennonites and is a delicious way to use apples. It can also be made with half pears to apples, but can take longer to thicken as pears do not have as much pectin as apples. This is really delicious on cheese scones, toast, or served with cheese, pork or chicken or stirred into yogurt. It is somewhere between jam and chutney, I guess ... The recipe is adaptable depending on how much fruit you have!

❧ Peel, core and chop all the apples you can fit into a large, heavy based pan. Add a little water or better yet, apple juice FT. Heat gently until all apples are soft and can be smooshed into apple sauce. Leave unsweetened; when cool, measure by liquid measurement, not by weight.

❧ Pour into your largest roasting tin sprayed with oil.

❧ Then, to each 1 litre (35 fl oz) of apple sauce, add caster sugar, cider vinegar, cinnamon and cloves.

❧ Stir completely and bake at 180°C (350°F) Gas 4 for 3 hours, or until thick. Stir every 20 minutes, scraping edges down into centre. It takes a good 2 hours to begin to go darker and get thicker; it needs 3 hours to really turn into 'butter'. Pour into jars* and seal.

To sterilise jars; wash jars and lids in really hot, soapy water, rinse well, place on an oven tray and put in the oven at 100°C (212°F) for 15 minutes; hopefully time this to when they are needed. Fill jars nearly to the top with chutney or apple butter or whatever you're making and screw on lids very tightly.

Evie's Mixed Fruit Chutney

A large preserving pan or stock pan; sterilised jars and lids*

1 teaspoon cloves FT

1 teaspoon peppercorns FT – tie these both in a muslin bag or closed tea strainer

110g (4oz) chopped apricots FT – cover with hot water for ½ hour, then drain

125g (4½oz) chopped organic dates FT

6 pears, chopped peeled and cored (we grow them at Lee Abbey)

6 small chopped red onions

2 tablespoons grated fresh root ginger

2 teaspoons sea salt

200g (7oz) brown sugar FT

625ml (20fl oz) vinegar (organic cider or red wine)

*See Apple Butter
(page 53)
for method to
sterilise jars and lids.
Hygiene is important!

Evie's Mixed Fruit Chutney

Former Tea Cottage worker Evie, from Poland – now married to an Englishman and living in Wales – was very good at creating chutney recipes using what we grew and what we had to hand and it was always delicious! Here is one of the best …

🌶 Cook all ingredients until thick; remove the bag of spices, pour into sterilised jars and seal.

🌶 This chutney is delicious straight away, but it is even better if kept for one month.

🌶 Label chutney and keep in fridge after opening.

🌶 Good for 12 months in sterilised jars.

Spiced Blackberry Chutney

Large preserving pan or stock pan

Sterilised jars and lids*

500g (1lb 2oz) blackberries

160g (5oz) caster sugar FT

160g (5oz) red onions, sliced

3 tablespoons chopped ginger or grated fresh root ginger

2 tablespoons Dijon mustard

salt and pepper FT to taste

150ml (5fl oz) red wine vinegar

*See Apple Butter (page 53) for method to sterilise jars and lids.

Spiced Blackberry Chutney

🍃 Combine all the ingredients except the vinegar in a large saucepan.

🍃 Over medium heat, cook until the blackberries burst, then season with a little salt and pepper.

🍃 Add the vinegar, and simmer uncovered for 10-20 minutes until thickened.

🍃 Cool slightly and pour into sterilised jars and seal.

🍃 It is possible to freeze blackberries as you have time to pick them and then defrost them all at once to make this chutney.

Red Onion Chutney

Large preserving pan
or stock pan

Sterilised jars and lids*

8 red onions, thinly sliced

110g (4oz)
caster sugar FT

80ml (3½fl oz)
red wine vinegar

80ml (3½fl oz)
red wine FT

1 clove of garlic chopped

2 whole cloves

2 teaspoons
ground cinnamon FT

2 tablespoons cranberry
or blackberry juice,
cordial or Ribena

*See Apple Butter
(page 53)
for method to
sterilise jars and lids.

Red Onion Chutney

🍎 Place the onions, sugar, garlic and spices into the preserving pan and cook for 10 minutes until soft (this will take longer if multiplying the recipe).

🍎 Add the vinegar and wine; simmer uncovered until sticky, for about 10 minutes. Add the juice, cooking a little longer till absorbed, stir and cool slightly; spoon into sterilised jars and seal.

This is yummy with cheese and great with sausages too. For a special party, chop sausages into bite-sized pieces, stick on a cocktail stick and add a tiny cherry tomato or black olive; arrange on a plate around a generous bowl of chutney for dipping. Also makes a excellent gift for foodie friends.

Spicy Apricot Fairtrade Chutney

Large preserving pan and sterilised jars and lids*

700g (1lb 8oz) dried apricots FT, chopped

110g (4oz) dried dates/ mango FT, chopped

440g (14oz) soft brown sugar FT

850ml (30fl oz) cider vinegar

3 medium onions, red or white, chopped small

150g (5oz) sultanas FT

5 tablespoons grated fresh root ginger

2 teaspoons dried ground ginger FT

3 teaspoons ground coriander

5 cloves garlic, chopped very small

2 level tablespoons sea salt

1 teaspoon cayenne pepper

grated zest and juice of 3 oranges FT

*See Apple Butter (page 53) for method to sterilise jars and lids.

Spicy Apricot Fairtrade Chutney

This sells out faster than we can make it and tastes pretty wonderful straight away, but is even better if kept for a month.

Place all the ingredients into the large pan and heat very gently, stirring until all the sugar is dissolved.

Raise heat to simmer and keep an eye on the chutney to avoid scorching. Simmer away for nearly an hour. The onion wants to still have shape and a little crunch, but the syrupy flavours want to be melded.

When it is shiny and cooked, scoop into sterilised jars and seal them up tight. Label before you forget what you've made and enjoy!

Delicious with sausages, hummus, cheese or scones; put on top of pâté, or leftover mashed potatoes for a different treat.

Tea Cottage Rhubarb Chutney

Large preserving pan or stock pan

Sterilised jars and lids*

675g (1lb 8oz) rhubarb, well rinsed and cut into chunks

270g (10oz) red onions, chopped small

270g (10oz) caster or granulated sugar FT

270ml (10fl oz) vinegar – cider, white wine or malt

2 tablespoons grated fresh root ginger

1 teaspoon cinnamon FT

zest of a large orange FT

handful of raisins/ sultanas FT

*See Apple Butter (page 53) for method to sterilise jars and lids.

Tea Cottage Rhubarb Chutney

🍎 Place **one third** of the vinegar and all the other ingredients in the pan and simmer over a low heat until the sugar is dissolved and the rhubarb soft.

🍎 Add the remaining vinegar and cook until desired consistency. Pot at once in sterilised jars and put on the lids tightly.

🍎 Label and keep in a cool dark place – good for 8 months or so.

🍎 Store in the fridge once opened.

This complements venison, game dishes and stir fries as well as the usual sausages/cheese/ham. You could try adding some curry powder/ cayenne pepper if you like spicy chutney.

If you have a glut of rhubarb, chop it into chunks and freeze, then just defrost when you want to make the chutney. It is a lovely pink colour when cooked. Sweet!

Tea Cottage Pear and Ginger Chutney

Large preserving pan
or stock pan

Sterilised jars and lids*

1.5kg (3lb) pears,
peeled and cored

500g (1lb) onions,
red or white, chopped

1 orange FT,
zest and juice

1 lemon FT, zest and juice

150g (5oz) sultanas
or raisins FT

250g (8oz)
caster sugar FT

3 cloves and 4
peppercorns FT tied
in muslin

2 tablespoons
grated fresh root ginger

2 teaspoons
ground dried ginger FT

¼ teaspoon salt

275 ml (10fl oz)
cider vinegar

*See Apple Butter
(page 53)
for method to
sterilise jars and lids.

Tea Cottage Pear and Ginger Chutney

🍎 Put all ingredients into a large preserving or stock pan and simmer until thick.

🍎 Remove the sachet of cloves/peppercorns and scoop into hot, sterilised jars and screw the lids on tightly.

🍎 Label and keep for a few weeks before serving. Good for 10 months or so in a cool dark place. Keep in fridge once opened.

🍎 This chutney is nice on toast topped with grated cheese and bubbled under the grill. We used our own pears that were fairly hard, but they made great chutney.

This recipe can be adapted to include half apples, or even a few plums and dates can be used instead of sultanas. Watch for too much sweetness and reduce the sugar if the fruit is very sweet or ripe.

Tea Cottage Fairtrade Hummus

1 jar light tahini FT

3 x 400g tins of chick peas (Americans call them garbanzo beans) drained but keep the liquid

juice of 2 lemons and zest (optional)

freshly ground black pepper FT

olive oil FT

2-4 cloves garlic

It's best to use unwaxed lemons if using the zest (see note on page 72).

Tea Cottage Fairtrade Hummus

A food processor or blender is pretty vital for making this.

Hummus came originally from the Middle East. Tahini is like peanut butter only it is made from sesame seeds. It comes dark or light. (I prefer the lighter one.) It is available in larger supermarkets or from the suppliers listed on page 75.

Put the chick peas (you can substitute one of the tins of chick peas with butter beans) and about ½ one tin of liquid in the processor. Blitz until ground but still slightly gritty. Add the jar of tahini, scraping all the good oil in. Add the garlic. Turn on the food processor and drizzle in about 1–2 tablespoons of olive oil.

Drizzle in half the lemon juice. Stop the machine, scrape the sides and grind in the pepper. Stir it around and taste. You can make it lighter by adding more of the bean liquid and sharper by more lemon juice. More oil is nice, but makes it more fattening. Go for the taste.

Now, if you want to add sun-dried tomatoes or caramelized onions, this is the time.

Serve with warm bread, or olives or strips of roasted peppers in a warm wrap.

Serve with a drizzle of good olive oil and a dash of paprika – try sweet smoked Spanish paprika.

This is vegan and very nutritious. Hummus can be frozen but allow several hours for it to defrost thoroughly.

Tea Cottage Smoothies

Obviously anyone can make a smoothie! You can buy them, but we started with wanting to use and promote some beautiful fruit puree from *Fruto del Spiritu* (www.fruto.co.uk) from Colombia in South America, with their UK representatives based in Essex.

These bottles of goodness help small-scale farmers export their unique and nutritious fruit. It keeps them making a living for themselves and their families, rather than having to resort to growing coca for cocaine. That is a great start. These fruits are really delicious and so versatile. We got straight on with developing ideas ...

My favourite is the Andean Blackberry, with various British summer fruits and maybe banana and Fairtrade apple juice. Others love the mango, or guava, mixed with

Fairtrade pineapple, melon and orange juice. We open the bottle and use some, then freeze the rest in ice cube trays, adding fruit to the cubes, these are then ready when anyone orders.

We also found freezing small chunks of fruit into fruit juice in ice cube trays worked beautifully when we had a large amount of punch to serve at a wedding reception. The fruit cubes slowly melted, adding colour and flavour as the punch was waiting to be drunk.

See the list of stockists on page 75 and try some at home. They apparently make good cocktails too, but we didn't feel that would be so appropriate at morning coffee time or with cream teas!

Elderflower Syrup

**Big, very clean bucket
Large saucepan**

1 litre (35fl oz) water

4 cups caster or granulated sugar FT (use a tea cup)

juice and zest of 2 lemons

2 tablespoons citric acid (from Brew shops)

15–25 elderflower heads
(check on the internet or in tree books to be certain of identifying the elderflowers you can use)

Remove flowers completely from stems and stalks. *(The stems are poisonous if eaten in large quantities so try to separate them as best you can.)*

Don't gather the flowers from busy road-sides, they will be dirty!

Elderflower Syrup

We made this one summer when the elderflowers coming out coincided with fewer customers because of rain ... It didn't happen that way again – when the garden is full of customers, you can't go out and leave them while you lean over hedges and climb fences to pick flowers!

*It is very delicious, especially made up with sparkling water.
Harriet Holmes helped advise us as did Pat Rogers, who both know about how to enjoy what grows around us.*

❧ Rinse the elderflowers to remove any dirt or insects etc.

❧ Snip off the flowers from the stalks into a large bowl or bucket that will hold everything. Add zested lemons, the citric acid and lemon juice.

❧ Bring the sugar and water to boil in a large saucepan, stirring to dissolve. Pour this syrup over the flowers etc. in the bucket. Stir to combine, cover with a towel and leave it for 2–4 days.

❧ After that, strain it through a very fine mesh sieve/strainer lined with muslin/cheesecloth into a sterilised bottle or large jar.

❧ Put on a clean lid and keep the syrup in the fridge. Try it with still or sparkling water or try drizzling over cake or yogurt. Yum! (Compost the flower heads of course.)

Smoked Mackerel Pâté

3 small smoked mackerel fillets (*peppered ones are alright, but it works best if you wipe off at least half of the pepper). The local honey smoked ones from Devon are divine.*

250g cream cheese

zest and juice of 1 lemon FT

freshly ground black pepper FT (unless they are peppered already)

1 teaspoon horseradish sauce

Smoked Mackerel Pâté

A food processor helps with this dish, but it can be done with a fork or small potato masher. It freezes well and is a delicious starter or light lunch. This pâte works well as a dip or topping for canapés.

🐚 **Remove skin and bones** from the fish. Of course the fresher the fish, the better the end result.

🐚 The lighter version of cream cheese can be used if desired, but my friend Sue Periam makes it with half whipped cream and it is great!

(If you live in Scotland, crowdie – a low fat soft cheese – makes a perfect substitute for the cream cheese and is lower in fat. Yum).

🐚 Smoosh all the fish and cream cheese together, stirring until smooth.

🐚 Add the lemon zest and half the lemon juice and the horseradish sauce. Taste and add the pepper and juice as needed.

🐚 Keeps in the fridge for 4 days or freeze on the day it is made. Serve with a dash of paprika or cayenne pepper on top.

Serve with bruchetta or a nice warm crusty roll, some peppery salad greens and a squeeze of lemon. You can use the same recipe with smoked salmon, especially the roasted type. Wow!

Homemade Guacamole

Make as little or much as you need, but these are the proportions:

1 large ripe avocado, peeled and chopped

juice of 1 lime (it works with lemon if you can't get a lime)

½ onion, red or white, chopped very small

½ red pepper, de-seeded and chopped small

salt and freshly ground black pepper FT

Homemade Guacamole

For Mexican food aficionados, this is a must, probably best with lots of added chillies! However, it can be made with less fire and is a fresh, tasty addition to chicken dishes, salads of all kinds and even spread on bread with cranberry and leftover turkey on Boxing Day.

❧ Start by squeezing the lime juice into a bowl. Using a fork, smoosh up the avocado into the juice and add the other ingredients, keeping it slightly chunky to add interest. Add salt and pepper to taste and now you can add either shop salsa, or fresh chillies to your own taste.

❧ Surprisingly, this keeps well if covered and in the fridge for about 3 days and can be frozen from fresh, ideal if all your avocados come ripe at once and it is not the day of your big Mexican Festival! It may go a bit brown but just stir it through. A dash of paprika or cayenne pepper on the top is very nice too.

❧ Serve with tortilla chips, or better yet spread tortilla chips on a baking tray, top with grated cheddar or other tasty cheese and grill for a few minutes till bubbled and going brown on the edges. Add chopped chillies if you like or just serve hot with the Guacamole. It is also very nice in a wrap with roasted peppers, onions and salsa.

Vinaigrette

Make it in a recycled jar and keep reusing

Choose a nice bottle or jar, clean it really well

½ jar of cider Vinegar – or your favourite. Try white wine vinegar, or blackberry, or rosemary infused, for a change!

mustard, a pinch of dry or a teaspoon of made-up

salt and pepper FT to taste

balsamic vinegar, a good tablespoon but optional

Any sugar FT, start with a teaspoon and add as needed, or honey FT

a clove or two of garlic, optional - crush, chop, or leave just bruised in the jar to infuse. (Don't be surprised when it turns green, it is ok)

oil – vegetable, rape seed or olive oil FT, try different types but get the best you can afford

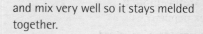

Vinaigrette

🐦 Add all the ingredients – except the oil – to the jar and shake very well, add:

🐦 ¼ oil – in other words, ¼ of the jar, so half the amount of vinegar you start with. Go on, get creative! Try with fresh herbs, or use a blender and mix very well so it stays melded together.

🐦 If it is too oily, add a small dash of vinegar. If too zingy, add a little more sugar. Olive oil FT is great, or try oil from various countries.

🐦 Shake again. Taste and season as needed, but sometimes simple is best.

🐦 Store in the fridge, but if using good quality olive oil FT, take out a little while before serving, as olive oil sets in the fridge.

This simple dressing is delicious on salads, over fish or chicken before grilling, or on veggie burgers or nut cutlets. Make it your own; let it become your signature dish ingredient.

Potato Salad

small new potatoes

mayonnaise

a little olive oil, sea salt
and freshly ground
black pepper

2 teaspoons of mustard
(we tried some nice
flavoured ones with
tarragon or honey!)

a splash of some
good vinegar

Potato Salad

🍂 Start with small new potatoes if in season. Cut them small or leave them chunky, but boil them until they are just cooked but still firm.

🍂 Cool slightly, add the ingredients and then chill completely. We vary our salads, mostly because it is a great place to learn to experiment and share ideas with other Team members.

🍂 Add a large serving spoon of mayonnaise per 800g of cooked, chopped potatoes. Add a little olive oil, sea salt, freshly ground black pepper, 2 teaspoons of mustard and then a splash of vinegar.

🍂 Some of the Team like to add chopped celery, others prefer to add only oil, vinegar, seasoning and chopped chives and various colours of chopped, de-seeded sweet peppers.

🍂 A very delicious idea is to add a small amount of mayonnaise and half a jar of rocket pesto. (We buy this from Essentials Co-op in Bristol and it is organic.) Wow, now **that** tastes fabulous either warm or cold!

Thanks to Billy Gerritson Rowe for this idea. She is such a great woman and cook and my son Caleb married her!

Tea Cottage 🍂 Lee Abbey Devon

Coleslaw

carrots

white or purple cabbage

eating apples

scoop of mayonnaise

pepper FT

splash of cider vinegar

several teaspoons
cinnamon FT

1 tablespoon
soft brown sugar FT

diced celery

dried cranberries

Coleslaw

🍎 Coleslaw – can be made with just carrots or white cabbage or even purple cabbage to be colourful. First, squeeze half a lemon into a bowl and chop up cored eating apples, leaving the skin on.

🍎 Add a scoop of mayonnaise to the sea salt and freshly ground black pepper FT, a splash of cider vinegar, several teaspoons cinnamon FT, a tablespoon of soft brown sugar FT, the juice and apples, and lots of diced celery. Then add the grated carrots and cabbage.

🍎 A good handful of dried cranberries tossed in at the end does add lovely colour and flavour. Rather American, I think. If nut allergies are not an issue this recipe takes well to adding chopped walnuts or slivered almonds FT.

**Tea Cottage Thyme
Infused Shallots**

Large stock pan and
sterilised jar(s) for
storage*

850g (2lb) shallots or
small pickling onions

2 tablespoons lemon
thyme leaves and a good
handful of sprigs

50ml (2fl oz)
balsamic vinegar

250ml (9fl oz) olive oil

Poaching liquor:

700ml (25fl oz)
white wine vinegar

700ml (25fl oz) water

1½ tablespoons sea salt

1½ tablespoons
caster sugar FT

a few sprigs of the lemon
thyme in the liquor

*See Apple Butter
(page 53)
for method to
sterilise jars and lids.*

Tea Cottage Thyme Infused Shallots

🌿 **Firstly,** peel the shallots. This can be made easier by boiling them in plain water for one minute, then chilling over very cold water (in a colander) and slipping off their skins. Leave the little points on.

🌿 Then, boil the poaching liquor to dissolve the salt and sugar. Add the shallots and bring back to the boil. Lower the temperature and simmer for 10 minutes. Drain them into a colander over a bowl, in case you want to re-use the liquor for a second batch and let them evaporate some of the liquid.

🌿 **Now,** put all the rest of the lemon thyme in the sterilised jars, fill with the cooked shallots and pour over the balsamic vinegar and olive oil and seal. If the oil does not cover the shallots, keep turning the jars to coat the shallots each time you pass them or when you open the fridge, where you can keep them once opened.

🌿 **However,** this was a luxury item we loved the taste of, but could not sustain production for serving every day. We discovered that if we bought the **top** of the range catering pickled onions and boiled them for one minute in the liquor they came in, plus lemon thyme and a little sugar; then threw out that liquor and put them back in their large, clean jars, with good balsamic and some olive oil and loads of our garden lemon thyme, they were a big improvement on the standard issue onions, saved us time (but not thyme?) and were that little bit more special.

🌿 If you have a cool place in your kitchen and use them often, keep them there, as in the fridge the olive oil will set. You could try making some dressing out of the oil and balsamic when the onions are all used up ...

Tea Cottage Fairtrade Marmalade with Ginger

one tin each of prepared oranges and lemons available in large supermarkets in the jam section.

juice and zest of:

3 lemons

2 limes

1 grapefruit

4 balls of 'ginger in syrup'

3 tablespoons of syrup from the jar

2 tablespoons of dried ginger FT

orange juice FT

caster sugar FT

*See Apple Butter (page 53) for method to sterilise jars and lids.

Tea Cottage Fairtrade Marmalade with Ginger

We found people really like buying whatever we produced in jars for them to take away, to remember their visit to the Tea Cottage and to support the work of Lee Abbey. So one day we decided to try making marmalade. Now don't be too impressed, we started with those **tins** of prepared oranges and lemons ... Shock! Horror! Not really homemade? But yes, we did quite a bit to those lowly Spanish prepared fruit. We added Fairtrade juice and the zest and juice of fresh citrus fruit. And we added lots of, you guessed it, ginger!

To each tin, (one tin of oranges and one tin of lemons) substitute fruit juice FT for half of water, in addition add the juice and zest of 3 lemons and 2 limes and one grapefruit;

Chop up about four balls of 'ginger in syrup' and add about 3 tablespoons of syrup from the jar. Add 2 tablespoons of dried ginger FT. Warming up there, are we?

Make it as per instructions on the tin and use sugar FT.

Pot up in recycled, sterilised* glass jars and presto, *Tea Cottage Fairtrade Three Fruit Marmalade with Ginger.*

Yummy and try it on scones, it nearly surpasses strawberry jam! This marmalade makes a perfect gift. And yes, in an ideal world we would make it from scratch, with Fairtrade oranges, Fairtrade juice and Fairtrade sugar and ginger. It is what we will aim for next season.

Helpful hints (with space to add your own)

🍃 When making a green salad with **iceberg lettuce**, tap the head of the lettuce hard on a board or edge of the sink and pull out the core, then tear the leaves without using a metal knife, thus preventing the lettuce going brown and rusting.

🍃 Buy **bananas** when they are cheap, or if extra ripe and peel and freeze in zip-lock bags and save for when you have time to make *Banana Bread*, (see page 42) cake or smoothies.

🍃 **Compost** all you can when preparing food, but save the apple and pear cores and peel for the birds if you have a bird table. Or make *Bird Cakes*, (see page 31).

🍃 A potato peeler makes excellent **chocolate curls.**

🍃 It is wise to crack each **egg** on a saucer before separating or adding to a recipe, just in case they are not fresh or the yolk breaks when separating the eggs for a recipe.

🍃 **Eggs** are marked at present with a 'Best Before Date'. However, quite often they are still usable after this date. This is the way to check them: fill a clear jug with cold water, place one raw egg (with shell on) at a time in the water and if it lies on its side or tilts, it is still safe to use. If it stands straight up, it is **off**. This is because as the egg ages, it absorbs more air, making the sack of air inside larger and therefore it stands up. So if it is lying it is good. If it stands up, throw it out!

🍃 The best way to peel the skin off fresh **root ginger** is to use a teaspoon.

🍃 **Burnt pans:** here is one pretty well proven way to clean off burnt ingredients, even when really burnt on: rinse off as much of the top layer and bits of ingredients as possible. Pour a cup full of bio laundry powder over the charred remains and roll around to coat every surface. Then top with boiling water and bring to the boil on the hob. **Watch** like the proverbial hawk, as it will boil up and **all over!** Just before it does that, switch off the heat and **leave it** for at least 4 hours, or overnight.

Hopefully this process will loosen most of the burnt ingredients, but further elbow grease may be required and sometimes only a wire wool scrubber will suffice. The joy of stainless steel pans is they can take the abuse. I am sorry to admit that the eco-friendly non-bio laundry powder does not do this job as well. Great on clothes, just not really nasty chemical enough to shift properly sacrificed potential yummy.

🍃 **Burnt ingredients**: on the issue of waste, I cannot stand it! So if you are making our Tea Cottage Fudge, or something similar to Scottish Tablet and it starts to burn, quickly take it off the heat and pour away the top portion that is not burnt into another clean pan.

This amount, if not yet tainted with a burnt taste and smell, can be cooked and finished as before, but obviously requiring a smaller tray for the end product. This works for Shortbread Millionaires/ Chocolate Caramel Shortbread, too. But don't cry, worse things happen at the Tea Cottage ...

 Choose unwaxed **lemons** if you are going to be zesting them, otherwise you are mostly zesting wax. Give them a good wash in hot water and to get the most juice out of a lemon/lime/orange, warm it very slightly in the microwave, then roll it, pressing down with your hand on a work surface to loosen the juicy bits from the skin.

Left over half **lemons** help cut grease when cleaning pans, just rub it all over and wash with less soap. Watch in the supermarkets for Fairtrade lemons and oranges. It is nice to think the farmers and pickers get a proper wage and price when we get good fruit.

Psalm 34 *as used for morning prayers*

I will always say good things about the LORD.
Every day my lips will sing psalms to him.

My soul will boast about the LORD.
Humble people will hear it. It will make them happy.

Let us all make people see that the LORD is great.
We will make his name famous together.

I prayed to the LORD and he answered me.
He saved me from everything that made me afraid.

Humble people looked to the LORD and were happy.
Their faces were not ashamed.

This humble man prayed and the LORD heard him.
The LORD took him away from all his troubles.

The angel of the LORD made a camp.
He stayed in it, round the people that feared the LORD.
He took them away from danger.

Oh, taste and see that the LORD is good.
The man that trusts in him will be very happy.

Oh, fear the LORD all his saints.
People that fear him will need nothing.

Young lions may need food and become hungry.
People that pray to the LORD will not need any good thing.

Children, come and listen to me.
I will teach you the fear of the LORD.

Which one of you finds pleasure in life?
Who wants time to see good things?

Do not say anything evil,
or let your lips tell anything that is false.

Turn away from evil and do good things.
Look for peace and follow it.

The LORD's face is against the people that do evil.
Nobody in all the earth will remember them.

The eyes of the LORD are on the righteous
and his ears listen when they pray.

The LORD hears them when they cry for help.
He saves them from all their troubles.

The LORD is near when their hearts break.
He saves those whose spirits are very sad.

Many evil things happen to the righteous,
but the LORD saves the righteous from them all.

The LORD keeps all their bones safe.
Not one of them becomes broken.

Evil things will kill very bad people.
The LORD will punish the people that hate righteous people.

The LORD will make his servants free
and not punish anyone that trusts him.

Some thoughts on Fairtrade at Lee Abbey ...

We seek to work out our faith in word and deed and this can hopefully be seen in many choices we make as Christians, concerning how we use our time, talents and resources.

At various times we have been asked about Sunday trading, a concern for some Christians. We, for example, sell our estate lamb and beef on a Sunday afternoon as guests are leaving, so it is freshly frozen for their journey.

The whole issue of how we honour God with Sabbath rest is a vital and whole other-book-full issue, but there are some important questions to ask about **trading** in the light of God's Kingdom. Does it matter what we sell, when we sell it and what price we charge? Is something more 'holy' if it has scripture printed on it, or features a Christian symbol? What would you say if you thought the majority of 'Christian' products sold in the UK are actually produced in China, with no ready acknowledgment of under what circumstances they are made?

As we attempt to choose Fairtrade at every level possible, we have to do a great deal of serious thinking about where we **buy** the things we sell and what our actions as a Christian charity say about the value we place on all people concerned. To quote

'Fairtrade is putting people back into the heart of trade and chipping away at deeply ingrained injustices.'

Harriet Lamb of the Fairtrade Foundation, 'Fairtrade is putting people back into the heart of trade and chipping away at deeply ingrained injustices.'

We at Lee Abbey serve the King of Kings, who cares deeply about the poor and oppressed. We believe that God came in the person of Jesus Christ to teach and enable us, by his death and resurrection, to follow his example. He sends his Holy Spirit to all who ask, so we may be empowered to live our lives full of mercy and justice. He teaches us to pray that his kingdom will come here on earth as it is in heaven and that his ways will flow like refreshing streams to all who thirst for truth. That kind of love is what drives us to serve others in all we do, think and say.

Suppliers for Fairtrade ingredients

Lee Abbey Shop: ask us if there is something in this book you can't find elsewhere and we may be able to get it for you.
▸ Email: shop@leeabbey.org.uk

Fair's Fair, Barnstaple, Devon: Helen and Roger Durant run the best Fairtrade shop I know. Full of beautiful and useful items, they know their stock and many of the suppliers. They carry a large range of food items and they support Fairtrade events at Lee Abbey. Coffee and homemade biscuits are available too.
Fair's Fair 17 Bear Street Barnstaple Devon EX32 7BX
Tel: 01271 370877

Fruto del Espiritu: for fruit puree, juices and dried fruits from South America via Essex.
www.fruto.co.uk

Griffin's Yard, South Molton, Devon: another local shop that carries many Fairtrade lines, cares about their customers and their producers. Nice craft shop too, and a cafe with great coffee and lunch.
Griffin's Yard North Road South Molton Devon EX36 3AZ
www.griffinsyard.co.uk
Tel: 01769 572372

Traidcraft: buy from a local Fairtrader who may sell from many churches/places of work/schools. Contact Traidcraft to find your nearest stockist. They can order for you and save you postage.
www.traidcraftshop.co.uk

Essential Trading: They are primarily a trade website, but contact them if you are trying to find a specific ingredient and they can help. The Tea Cottage buys their Rocket Pesto, organic flours, nuts and beans from them, as well as many other items they sell in the shop.
www.essential-trading.coop

The Co-op Supermarkets: are the best for a huge range of fairly traded ingredients. Also try Waitrose, Sainsburys and some larger Tesco and Asda stores. Always tell the staff in the store that you want more Fairtrade goods and that you came especially to look for them. If where you regularly shop does not stock many lines, tell them you are planning to go elsewhere!

Steenbergs: are the tea and spice people who linked me up to the growers in Sri Lanka. They are now offering many more lines of fairly-traded organic and other whole food items online. This is a great site and a good place to start looking for newly certified fairly-traded goods and quality products from an excellent company.
www.steenbergs.co.uk

Tea Cottage   Lee Abbey Devon

Thank you

This cookery book is the work of everyone who has served at the Tea Cottage at Lee Abbey, especially since 2009. I would like to especially thank:

The Lee Abbey Maintenance Team for their honest feedback and sample eating each spring, which I know they pretend to dread, but really love.

Thank you to all our guests.

Inspiration for creating good food that cares about everyone in the process comes significantly for me from Delia Smith and Doris Janzen Longacre, who wrote the *More with Less Cookbook*, a Mennonite Central Committee publication, full of incredible insights into the global food situation.

I have also been greatly influenced and encouraged by Helen Durant, Sue Periam, Sue and Andrew Redbond, Janie Morgan, Sheila Marlow and Cathy Park.

Thank you to my mother, Nancy Mason Paris, dad, Marshall Paris, sister, Mary Clare Paris, brothers, George, Peter and Patrick Paris, our children, Melissa Rowe Baker and Esther Rowe, Billy Gerritson Rowe and Caleb Rowe, Agi Szilagyi Rowe and Jesse Rowe, Ian Baker, sister in law Suzanne Rowe Hodgson, and my beloved husband, David B. Rowe.

Thank you to Sarah Prentice for her gifted design and belief in this project. James and Inger Denniston, Claire Painting, Sophie Davis, Stuart, Caroline and Eden Townend, Andrew Mann, Alan Johnson, Kate Robinson and Phil and Maddy Crook.